ALL VERSIONS OF ME THAT EXISTS

ADDING MEANING TO LIFE

ZUNERIA FATIMA

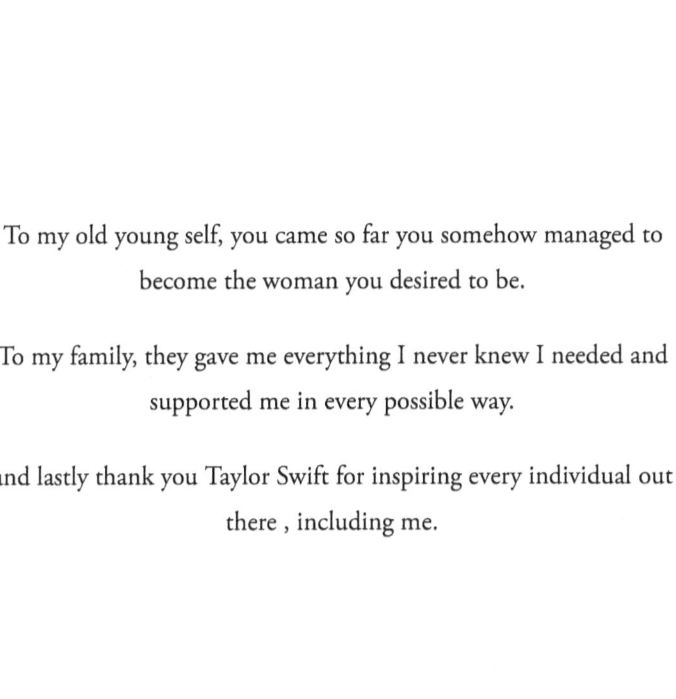

To my old young self, you came so far you somehow managed to become the woman you desired to be.

To my family, they gave me everything I never knew I needed and supported me in every possible way.

and lastly thank you Taylor Swift for inspiring every individual out there , including me.

Contents

Foreword   *vii*

Preface   *ix*

Acknowledgements   *xi*

Prologue   *xiii*

Table Of Contents   *xvii*

A Girl Who Loves Living

Better Discussion

Be Who You Want To Be

Part 4

Part 5

Feminine

All I Find Myself

Part 8

Part 9

Part 10

Just Another Lost Angel

Still Holding On

Part 13

Part 14

Part 15

The Idea Of Others Loving Us

The Only Way Out Is Through

I Knew I Would

She

Contents

Falling Apart

The Heart Healer

Part 22

All I Find Myself Loving

Going To Know More In The Future

18

Part 26

Part 27

About The Author   55

Foreword

As since I was a child I always love the art of poetry and so I did write this foreword.

The way the author portraited the poetry filled with a sense of emotions is beyond words.

I loved the way the author portraited the art of poetry. The book is about a person going through their life with a sense of touch and vulnerability. The book will make you love yourself a little more.

Each poem and prose is written with a full feeling of joy.

Preface

Poems on various subjects written at different rent times and prompted by very different feelings;

but when read under the influence of reading a poem- this will generate a love for poetry. The poet

developed her own fentiments and emotions through this form of art.

In my book, I discussed both the happy side of life as well as sad part of the life, which a Poet may rationally endeavour to impart.

Acknowledgements

As much as I'd just love to take all the credits for this book, so I'd like to thank everyone who contributed to my amazing life. And I am really grateful for my lifeto inspire me to consider new ideas throughout and made me a better version of myself each passing day.

To my Parents: Thank you for making me enough capable to write a book. You inspire and encourage me in so many ways. They loved me even on those days when I am easy to love.

Prologue

I write what I see

    I write what I experience

    I write what I love

15-05-2022

First edition: May 2022

Table Of Contents

A girl who loves living 1

Better Discussion 2

Be who you want to be 3

Fourth poem title 4

Fifth poem title 5

Feminine 6

All I find myself 7

Eighth poem title 8

Ninth poem title 9

Tenth poem title 10

Just another lost angel 11

Still holding on 12

Thirteenth poem title 13

Fourteenth poem title 14

Fifteenth poem title 15

The idea of others loving us 16

The only way out is through 17

I knew I would 18

She 19

Falling Apart 20

The Heart Healer 21

Twenty-Second poem title 22

All I find myself loving 23

Going to know more in the future 24

TABLE OF CONTENTS

18 25

Twenty-Sixth poem title 26

Twenty-Seventh poem title 27

A Girl who loves living

The sparks in her eyes was saying a lot

speaks through pen

Bleeds through paper

Thoughts running through mind as caper

So she wrote all it down as it was her work

Her aura is made up of poetries and roses

that's why she loves sad proses

Better Discussion

When I was all alone

I claimed myself for all the fears and worries I own

Someone said that"What you are going through is what you may already been through"

Just focus on the good deeds you had

I somehow felt

used to be a little kid with excitement and enthusiasm in the eye

Enjoys every single moments so hard that it turns out amazing.

My eyes gazed over the life of joy

Wanna go out and enjoy

thoughts breaking through mind

Full of keenness and kind

makes a human erudite

Be who you want to be

Be a poet who writes about life

Be a song writer who writes songs about love

Be a human with a kind heart full of cherishing joy

Be who you want to be

THE KIND OF RADIANCE SHE ONLY HAVE AT

SEVENTEEN

~ TAYLOR SWIFT

Don't live for being loved, live for love for yourself.

Don't let your energy waste on people who doesn't even know it's you who was making them loved.

Feminine

*But she is who nobody can imagine how strongly, feminine woman she
is*

but she is who cries over her scars but later on loved it the most.

All I find myself

I remember each and every detail of me others admires

From the innocence I have to the girl who loves poetry

Each and every beautiful quotes I read gave the idea of following a path of becoming naive

So unrealistic expectations set

Don't wanna settle for less until and unless I found the imperfect 'perfect'

Sleeps that gives the most beautiful dreams

when welcomes the reality is different, so I write another poem to persist.

Don't let anyone define you

It's you who can only choose to define yourself beautifully,

others may not

I write words and quotes with my pen and ink,

to express my emotions filled with my sorrow and kink

She's happy

She's good

She's trying

and she's me

Just another lost angel

I was in a nightmare without a night

I was in a crowd but still alone

a person with dreams ready to fight

As it was a story of a delinquent who lived on her own

Still holding on

Flashback waking up

Getting harder when it was already enough

Came into that sight again

Hearts arching, eyes pricking

Why there is sadness in this happiness?

The fear that I had come far away

I kept on weaving

Why I am still on that very first chapter when the exam has been
over?

Maybe it's the time of the month that ends without a pause

I know it's sad, but this is what I think about a lot more.

I wish I could give little me a hug

and just hold her

She did need me in her life way before

But for now I am happy for her because she came so far

cause now she is me.

There was a storm before me

But there will be calm because of me

There will be happiness after me

but there was also happiness because of me

And I believe everything gonna worth it

There will always be something that are harder to forget than to leave.

The idea of others loving us

We often search for people's validation into our work,

We dislikes the idea of self loving even though we're completely doing good.

We like to be looked according to society's beauty standard, this made us believe it's an art work.

But at the end of the day all you need is a good mood and a good food.

The only way out is through

Holding on too tight empties in between

Keeping it aside and being vulnerable and keen

Though it some time to survive it all

An unshakeable ally

Her eyes told million stories but they were too simple to be
understood

The scar was there

but I was the whole

It meant to be fixed out here

After multiple hallucinations and numerous delusions,

here I am still

It's ok to bring out what lies inside of you

At the end it will always be you

On the breezes of the sky

Wondering if I would fall or fly?

Silence and Sound

Screams and dreams

In search of healing

Maybe they had to take sometime

Learning to learn and

I still gotten that faith even now

Cause something about life feels a new beginning somehow

I knew I would

I knew I would be happy again

For things I knew I could save

Apparantly can't see the misogynous way

But wanna live with success of cuddles

Even if it is not known in puddles

She

She who wanted to be a poet but,

Deep down she was a poem

She handles pain,

that she's amazing

She's like a meadow flower

Unapologetically herself, that's her real superpower

A simple girl but far too complex to define

She's like phoenix: she always rises from the ashes to shine

And one day the girl with the books

became the women writing them

She writes her own stories'

Making each step flawless inspite of the flaws

She looks like fairies

the innocence she had

is for forever

A pure heart that never lied

She's a girl who loves to dance instead of walking

She's a girl who loves to sing instead of speaking

She loves to live instead of surviving

And yet she loves to become who she is becoming.

Falling apart

I always knew I was that charm

who could light up anything with the sparkle in my eye

Seems like that faded away, sighs'

Wanna spoken out

But all I feel day by day

Is to be serene, the way

I tried to be strong,

But don't know what went wrong.

The Heart Healer

Sometimes I feel like I am a heart healer

But who heals the heart healer?

People come and leave

It's the heart that stays

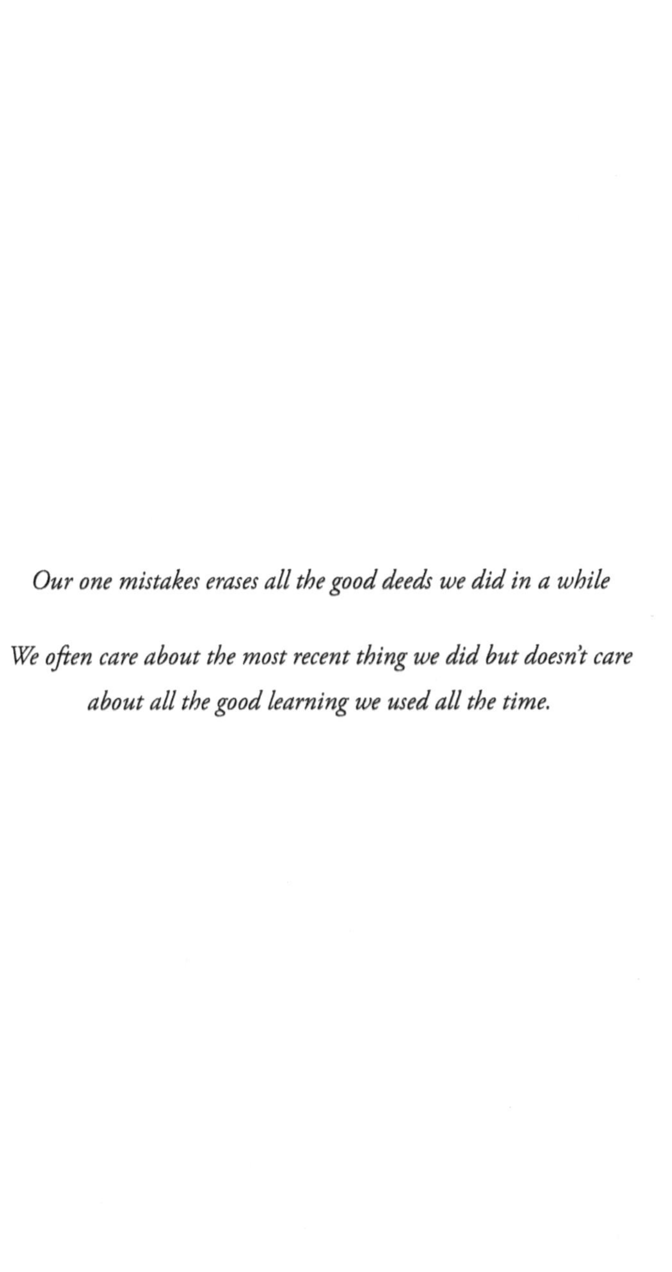

Our one mistakes erases all the good deeds we did in a while

We often care about the most recent thing we did but doesn't care about all the good learning we used all the time.

All I find myself loving

Let love heal all your wounds

*Collecting each and every piece of your broken soul enclosed in a
pound*

Fly high

Till you feel the need of wings to rely

The opportunity might be right out there

But you are strucked in a place called 'here'

Going to know more in the future

One asked 'Am I enough'?

Accepting yourself maybe tough

The inaccessible and unconscious of the soul

Not letting anything maul

Illusion shielding us from the ocean of despair

Between all that grief

We learnt to learn in brief

Life-long lessons managed to stay somehow

Figuring it out and giving a blast flow

But there no other love if there's no self love

My heart didn't need to be fixed

My heart needed to be loved

Loved by me

I have never started a new poem whose end i knew

but sometimes it's our task to discover something new

An ancestral concept

very few accept

Souls that feels bare

needs great worth to share

18

18 years of living and still couldn't figured out what went wrong

Pain may kill you but if once you get healed you become strong

Now the only years left

Is to be spent avoiding the pain of age?

It was supposed to be fun turning 18

But more likely to become sixteen again

Time flies

The only thing that remains constant is you

Comparison goes on

Rascism goes on

They revolve around it like a spin

*Even though they say a Person's heart is important but then goes on
checking the shade of skin.*

<u>When the sun rises the hope ultimately rises against the night-blue sky</u>

<u>Which depends upon an enormous sparks reflected in the eye</u>

<u>So reminds yourself on the greyest of the days</u>

<u>To become more serene again</u>

<u>For being bathed in its golden rays</u>

<u>Even if it's showering all pain</u>

<u>Let yourself remind of the storms that you already seen</u>

<u>Fill yourself with all the keen</u>

A person without a fear is a person who the world cheer.

About The Author

Zuneria Fatima is a published Indian Author and a student of Science. She wants her work to reach through people in the form of poetry. She loves writing new poem each day. The Book "All versions of me that exists" is her first book.

The idea of this book came unexpectedly; watching life passing each day made the set of poems turns into a book.

This book represents some of the tears I couldn't cry, some of the fears I had. This book is all about the versions of thoughts that co-exists.